Danielle Steel

EXPECT A MIRACLE

QUOTATIONS
TO LIVE AND
LOVE BY

MACMILLAN

To my children,
Beatrix, Trevor, Todd, Nick, Samantha,
Victoria, Vanessa, Maxx, and Zara

To the Special People I have loved

And to all of you,
who have been happy or sad,
who have known great joy or loss,
who are lonely or have lost hope,
or are scared and in despair,
or need a good laugh—We all do!

May the words that bring me
comfort and hope
help you too!

with all my love,

d. s.

Introduction

When I was a very young girl, about thirteen, my grandmother gave me a beautiful antique book with an embroidered cover and blank pages inside. I wasn't quite sure what to do with it. Write a story? Do drawings? I was more inclined to draw than to write. Then I began to find quotes I liked, wise words, often about love and the alleged meaning of life. And I began writing the sayings down in the book. It took me years to fill it. None of it was written in my own words; they were all quotations of other people's wisdom. I would read through the book from time to time, and loved what I had gathered.

The habit of collecting quotations stayed with me. I would find sayings that I liked, even anonymous ones, clip them out of magazines or greeting cards, and save them. I didn't research the sources or seek to verify them. It was the message that was meaningful, and I accepted the attributions. The wisdom of the words was what touched me. Sometimes I would make collages of them and give them to friends. Eventually I began framing the quotations, in several languages, and hanging them on my walls. I hang them mostly around my desk and the places where I work, even above my computer. I put them there so that on a bad day, I can look up and see something inspiring, or something that makes me laugh, to lighten the burdens and challenges of the day.

I suppose it's not surprising that I'm in love with words and always have been. I make collages, fill little notebooks with sayings that I like. I do artwork, using vintage letters to make a word that's meaningful to me. I love paintings and sculptures with words in them, and jewelry made with words, either in the form of a word or with words engraved on them. Words have become my career and my life, and my inspiration.

The right words can bring you back to reality or make you dream, can comfort you when you're in despair or make you laugh out loud. The right words can open your mind or give you hope. I use the quotations I save and frame to do just that: to remind me of what I need to know, that life is not as bleak as it appears sometimes, that there is always hope, and love, and joy. The right words give me courage, strength, and peace.

I hope that some of these sayings that I cherish (or that

make me laugh) will be the right words for you and give you just what you need at the right time. Please take them in the spirit I offer them to you, with love, as I share with you these words that have brought me great warmth and comfort.

Believe in miracles. Expect a miracle. Miracles DO happen, just as the quotations say. Life is a miracle, friendship is a miracle, laughter is a miracle, and so is love.

And I hope that these words touch your heart and make you smile.

love, Danielle

A ROA
TO

D MAP
LIFE

MIRA

D

HAP

CLES

PEN.

LIFE IS
A SERIES *of*
THOUSANDS
of TINY
MIRACLES.

MIKE GREENBERG

One of the deep secrets of life is that all that is really worth doing is what we do for others.

LEWIS CARROLL

Only a life lived for others is a life worthwhile.

ALBERT EINSTEIN

A thousand words will not leave so deep an impression as one deed.

HENRIK IBSEN

It is the
history
of our
kindnesses
that alone
makes this
world
tolerable.

✳

ROBERT LOUIS STEVENSON

*No act of
kindness,
however
small,
is ever
wasted.*

AESOP

THREE THINGS IN HUMAN LIFE ARE IMPORTANT.

✳

The first is
to be kind.
The second is
to be kind.
And the third is
to be kind.

HENRY JAMES

There is
no set path;
just follow
your heart.

We own
no future,
only

no past,
we possess
now.

MARY BAKER EDDY

Don't get so

making

you forget to

busy
a living that
make a life.

DOLLY PARTON

The construction of your life begins with accountability.

MITCH JONES

Believe in the power of believing in yourself.

Be the change you wish to see in the world.

ATTRIBUTED TO MAHATMA GANDHI

*DARE
TO BE
REMARKABLE!*

Bloom
where
you are
planted.

✳

ST. FRANCIS DE SALES

DO NOW WHAT YOU CAN'T DO LATER.

Life consists
not in holding
good cards
but in playing
those you
hold well.

JOSH BILLINGS

LIVE THE
PRESENT,
DREAM FOR THE
FUTURE,
LEARN FROM THE
PAST.

Do what you can,
with what you've got,
where you are.

THEODORE ROOSEVELT,
QUOTING SQUIRE BILL WIDENER

Life isn't about finding yourself, it is about creating yourself.

✳

COMMONLY ATTRIBUTED
TO GEORGE BERNARD SHAW

You are here **enable the** **more amply,** **vision, with a** **of hope and** **You are here** **the world.**

in order to
world to live
with greater
finer spirit
achievement.
to enrich

WOODROW WILSON

There is
a magic
about you
that is all
your own.

D. M. DELLINGER

*Life faces you with
courageous challenges
at every step of the way.
You are on the path, exactly
where you are meant to be
right now ... and from here,
you can only go forward,
shaping your life story into
a magnificent tale of triumph,
of healing, of courage,
of beauty, of wisdom, of
power, of dignity, of love.*

JANET ERSKINE STUART, RSCJ

It is

too late

your life

*never
to start
over.*

WHY

NOT?

I have the power to transform my life.

IF YOU CAN DREAM IT, YOU CAN DO IT.

TOM FITZGERALD,
DISNEY IMAGINEER

Never be
afraid to try
something new.
Remember,
amateurs built
the Ark,
professionals
built the Titanic.

✴

All things are difficult before they are easy.

THOMAS FULLER

Wherever you go, go with all your heart.

ATTRIBUTED TO
CONFUCIUS

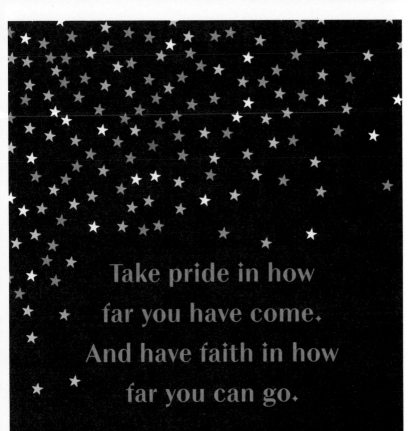

Take pride in how
far you have come.
And have faith in how
far you can go.

CHRISTIAN D. LARSON

*Be happy
for this
moment...
this moment
is your life.*

OMAR KHAYYAM

All human
wisdom
is contained
in these
two words:
Wait and Hope!

✷

ALEXANDRE DUMAS

Let your
LIGHT

SHINE!

Be
gentle
with
yourself.

MAX EHRMANN

SEIZE
THE
DAY!

Go forth and set the world on fire.

ST. IGNATIUS OF LOYOLA

Expect a
mir

acle.

FAI

TH

*Dear God,
be good to me.
The sea is so wide,
and my boat is
so small.*

**BRETON FISHERMAN'S
PRAYER**

GOD LEADS MEN
INTO DEEP WATER,
NOT TO DROWN THEM,
BUT TO CLEANSE THEM.

JOHN H. AUGHEY

Nothing is impossible to God.

MARY BAKER EDDY

God hath not given us the spirit of fear, but of power and of love, and of a sound mind.

✳

2 TIMOTHY 1:7

*Trust in the
Lord with all
thine heart;
and lean not
unto thine own
understanding.
In all thy ways
acknowledge
him, and he
shall direct thy
paths.*

✳

PROVERBS 3:5-6

Fear thou not; for I am with thee.

ISAIAH 41:10

GOD
IS
LOVE.

1 JOHN 4:8

Whatever blesses one blesses all.

MARY BAKER EDDY

God is never helpless.

God
has a
beautiful
plan.

God will open the way.

Divine Love always has met and always will meet every human need.

MARY BAKER EDDY

God setteth the solitary in families.

PSALM 68:6

In God,
who is the
source of
my strength,
I have the
strength for
everything.

✳

PHILIPPIANS 4:13

The
will
you

truth set free.

JOHN 8:32

*Every saint
has a past,
and every
sinner
has a future.*

OSCAR WILDE

Grant me the serenity
to accept the things
I cannot change,
the courage to change
the things I can,
and the wisdom
to know
the difference.

REINHOLD NIEBUHR,
SERENITY PRAYER

Dear God,
Instead of letting
people die and having
to make new ones
why don't you just
keep the ones
you got now?

JANE

(FROM *CHILDREN'S LETTERS*
TO GOD BY STUART HAMPLE
AND ERIC MARSHALL)

Dear God,
In Bible Times,
did they really
talk that fancy?

JENNIFER

(FROM *CHILDREN'S LETTERS
TO GOD* BY STUART HAMPLE
AND ERIC MARSHALL)

No one allowed the

will be
to miss
boat.

If the only

say your

is Thank

would

prayer you
whole life
You, that
suffice.

*

ATTRIBUTED TO MEISTER ECKHART

BELIE
MIRA

VE IN

CLES.

COUP

RAGE

✳

Courage is
not the absence
of fear or despair,
but the strength to
conquer them.

✳

Throughout the centuries there were men who took first steps down new roads armed with nothing but their own vision.

AYN RAND

Courage,
is nothing less
to overcome
misfortune, fear,
continuing to
that life with
is good.

it would seem,
than the power
danger,
injustice, while
affirm inwardly
all its sorrows

*

DOROTHY THOMPSON

I have the grace I need for today. I am full of power, strength, and determination. Nothing I face will be too much for me. I will overcome every obstacle, outlast every challenge, and come through every difficulty better off than I was before.

REV. JOEL OSTEEN

Believe in yourself
and all that you are.
Know that there is
something inside
you that is greater
than any obstacle.

CHRISTIAN D. LARSON

I will not talk
how big my
I will talk to
about how

to God about
problems are.
my problems
big my God is.

REV. JOEL OSTEEN

When you
go through a
disappointment,
when you go
through a loss,
don't stop on
that page.

REV. JOEL OSTEEN

Bounce back.

We wait for God to act. Maybe God is waiting for us to act.

REV. CECIL WILLIAMS

Give us grace and strength to
forbear and to persevere.
Give us courage and gaiety
and the quiet mind.
Spare to us our friends and
soften to us our enemies . . .
Give us the strength to
encounter that which is to
come, that we may be brave
in peril, constant in
tribulation, temperate in wrath,
and in all changes
of fortune, and down to the
gates of death, loyal
and loving to one another.

✳

ROBERT LOUIS STEVENSON

It has been said

"time heals all wounds."

I do not agree.

The wounds remain.

In time, the mind,

protecting its sanity,

covers them with scar tissue

and the pain lessens.

But it is never gone.

ROSE KENNEDY

If you're going through hell, keep going.

ATTRIBUTED TO WINSTON CHURCHILL

The night is darkest

before the dawn.

You can only be brave if you try what you're afraid of.

*Never give up,
never give up,
never,
never, never,
never give up.*

WINSTON CHURCHILL

*Just when
the caterpillar
thought the
world was over,
it became
a butterfly.*

THERE WILL

WHEN YOU

EVERYTHING

THAT WILL BE

COME A TIME
BELIEVE
IS FINISHED.
THE BEGINNING.

LOUIS L'AMOUR

LAUG

HTER

Chocolate is the answer. The question is pretty much irrelevant.

*Never fear
being vulgar,
only boring.*

DIANA VREELAND

*Behind every great woman
is a man checking out
her ass.*

The older you get, the better you get, unless you're a banana.

ROSE

(PLAYED BY BETTY WHITE),
THE GOLDEN GIRLS

Dear God,
I went to this
wedding, and
they kissed
right in church.
Is that OK?

✳

NEIL

(FROM *CHILDREN'S LETTERS*
TO GOD BY STUART HAMPLE
AND ERIC MARSHALL)

**Dear God,
Please put another
holiday between
Christmas and Easter.
There is nothing
good in there now.**

GINNY

(FROM *CHILDREN'S LETTERS*
TO GOD BY STUART HAMPLE
AND ERIC MARSHALL)

Dear God,
If we come back as something, please don't let me be Jennifer Horton because I hate her.

DENISE

(FROM *CHILDREN'S LETTERS TO GOD* BY STUART HAMPLE AND ERIC MARSHALL)

Dear God,
I bet it's very hard for
you to love all of
everybody in the whole
world. There are only
four people in our family,
and I can never do it.

NAN

(FROM *CHILDREN'S LETTERS*
TO GOD BY STUART HAMPLE
AND ERIC MARSHALL)

LO

VE

CHO
LO

OSE

VE!

NOTHING

DONE OR

THROUGH

IS

THAT IS
SUFFERED
LOVE
USELESS.

✴

GASTON COURTOIS

It is so much friendlier

with two.   SAID BY WINNIE-THE-POOH
TO PIGLET, *WINNIE-THE-POOH*

The measure of love is to love without measure.

✳

ST. FRANCIS DE SALES

A good
marriage
consists of
two good
forgivers.

RUTH BELL GRAHAM

THE ONLY
TOLD YOU
I LIKED
I ALREADY
LOVED

LIE I EVER IS THAT YOU WHEN KNEW I YOU.

THE L.A.-BASED STREET ARTIST
KNOWN AS WRDSMTH

Love has
no age.

FRENCH PROVERB

Love never fails.

Love demands everything, and rightly so.

LUDWIG VAN BEETHOVEN

Just live love—be it—
love, love, love.
Do not know anything
but love. Be all love.
There is nothing else.

✴

ATTRIBUTED TO
MARY BAKER EDDY

I STILL

IN SPITE OF

THAT

ARE TRULY

AT

BELIEVE, EVERYTHING, PEOPLE GOOD HEART.

ANNE FRANK

*One cannot
do big things,
only small ones,
with immense love.*

MOTHER TERESA

It is only with one's heart that one can see clearly. What is essential is invisible to the eye.

ANTOINE DE SAINT-EXUPÉRY,

THE LITTLE PRINCE

The best and
beautiful
world cannot
or even
They must
with

most
things in the
be seen
touched.
be felt
the heart.

ATTRIBUTED TO HELEN KELLER

You will be unique
in the world to me,
and I will be unique
in the world to you.

ANTOINE DE SAINT-EXUPÉRY,
THE LITTLE PRINCE

Whatever the question, love is the answer.

Believe in happy endings.

Here is a place to write and keep the quotes that bring you comfort, joy, and laughter, too.

_____

_____

_____

_____

_____

_____

_____

_____

_____

_____

_____

_____

_____

_____

_____

_____

_____

First published 2020 by Clarkson Potter, an imprint of Random House,
a division of Penguin Random House LLC, New York

First published in the UK 2020 by Macmillan
an imprint of Pan Macmillan
The Smithson, 6 Briset Street, London EC1M 5NR
Associated companies throughout the world
www.panmacmillan.com

ISBN 978-1-5290-4113-2

9 8 7 6 5 4 3 2 1

A CIP catalogue record for this book is available from the British Library.

Printed and bound by 1010 International Printing Ltd

Visit www.panmacmillan.com to read more about all our books
and to buy them. You will also find features, author interviews and
news of any author events, and you can sign up for e-newsletters
so that you're always first to hear about our new releases.